find out about diggers and cranes

Written by
Sally Hewitt and Nicola Wright

Designed by
Chris Leishman

Illustrated by
Rachael O'Neill

Contents

Chrysalis Education

Backhoe loader

The backhoe loader is two machines in one. It does some jobs with the hoe at the back, and other jobs with the loader at the front.

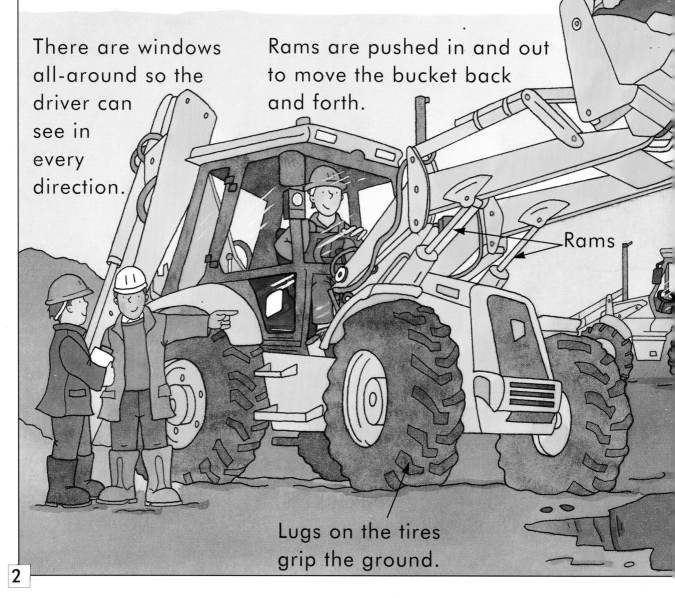

There are windows all-around so the driver can see in every direction.

Rams are pushed in and out to move the bucket back and forth.

Rams

Lugs on the tires grip the ground.

Special features

Bucket

The driver's seat can turn around to face the front or the back.

Arm

Backhoe

Stabilizers keep the machine steady while it is digging.

The loader bucket has strong metal teeth for digging.

The bucket can also split in half to grab piles of soil.

The backhoe arm can lift up and down, reach out and pull in.

3

Excavators

Excavators are digging machines. Each of these excavators does a special sort of digging job.

Backhoe

Split bucket

Hammer

Breaking hammer
The vibritory or hydraulic hammer is used to break up rocks and concrete.

Crawler tracks

Blade

Bulldozer
A bulldozer uses a heavy metal blade to clear the ground of rocks.

Grapple bucket

A grapple bucket opens and shuts like a mouth to bite into the earth.

Shovel

This special backhoe can swivel around to dig at the back, front, or on either side.

Mini excavators and mini loaders are specially made to work in small spaces.

Mini skiploader

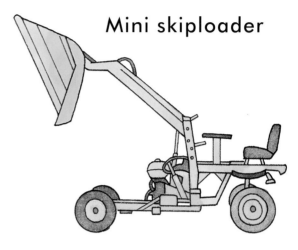

Mini excavator
with bucket and crawler tracks

Giant excavators

Rocks and stones used for building are dug out of quarries. The biggest excavators of all do this work.
They are called dragline excavators.

A dragline bucket is so big that a car could drive into it!

The enormous bucket scoops up huge amounts of rock.

Draglines are the wires that drag the bucket along the ground so that it fills up with rocks.

Some excavators can walk backward and forward on big metal pieces called shoes.

Quarrying cuts huge holes in the earth. Dragline excavators can also be used to fill the holes in again!

On the farm

Tractors with powerful engines and big wheels are very useful on farms. They can pull many different kinds of farm machines. All these machines get the ground ready for sowing seeds.

Tractor

Plow
A plow has sharp blades called plowshares. They dig into the soil and turn it over.

Plowshares

Roller
A roller smooths the soil and makes the field level.

Harrow
A harrow has rows of metal discs that cut the soil up into small pieces.

←Metal discs

Seed drill

This is used to plant seeds in fields.

Hopper

Spikes

Furrows ——→

First the drill makes lines, called furrows, in the soil.

Seeds pass out of the hopper, down the drills into the furrows.

Spikes pull soil over the seeds.

9

Road building

The ground has to be cleared and flattened before a new road can be built. All these machines work together to do the job.

Compactor
Compactors drive up and down flattening the ground.

Blade

Metal feet

Blade

Grader
Graders use a blade to smooth over the surface.

Wheels

Blades

Scraper
Scrapers scrape away small bumps.

Bulldozer
Bulldozers clear big obstacles out of the way.

The scraper blade is lowered to the ground. A trap door lifts as it collects a load. When full the load is pushed out from the back.

Compactors have heavy metal wheels covered in spikes called feet. They push down into the soil.

Graders have long blades. They spread out small stones in an even layer.

Mining

Mining machines dig tunnels and cut coal, or metals such as gold, from deep under the ground.

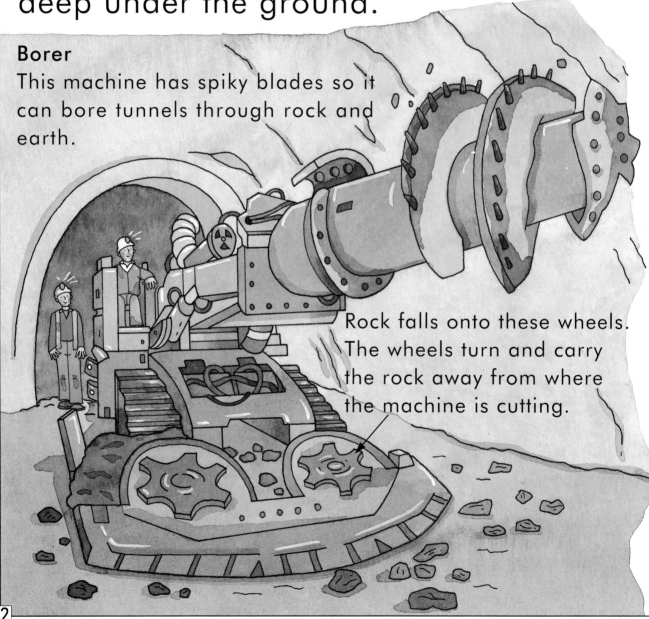

Borer
This machine has spiky blades so it can bore tunnels through rock and earth.

Rock falls onto these wheels. The wheels turn and carry the rock away from where the machine is cutting.

Coal-face cutter

This coal-face cutter moves along the tunnel, cutting off coal from the wall of the mine.

Coal face

Blades

Fun Fact

Once all the coal is removed, the tunnel is allowed to collapse.

Roof supports strengthen the roof and walls of the tunnel so they do not fall in.

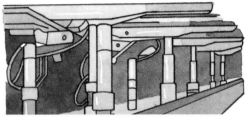

A **conveyor belt** carries the coal out of the tunnel.

Water sprays out of the coal cutter to damp down the coal dust.

Tunneling

This giant tunnel-boring machine is called a TBM. TBMs were used to cut through rock to build the Channel Tunnel under the sea between England and France.

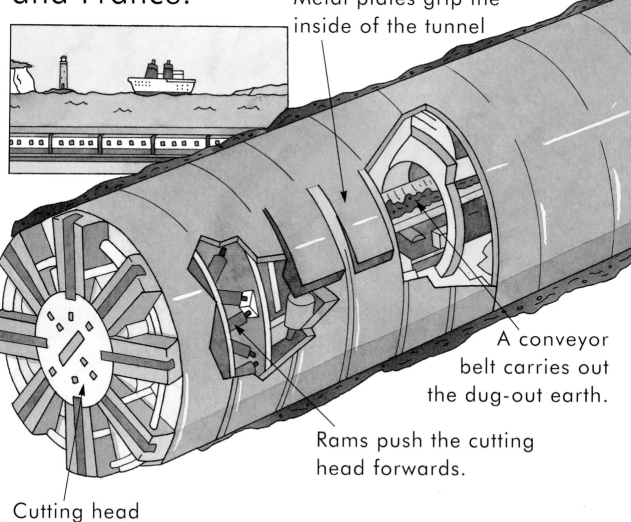

Metal plates grip the inside of the tunnel

A conveyor belt carries out the dug-out earth.

Rams push the cutting head forwards.

Cutting head

Concrete segments cover the inside of the tunnel.

The TBM control cabin has television cameras and computers.

Cutting head

This works like a drill. **Rams** push it against the rock. A big electric **motor** turns it round.

The huge cutting head can cut 12 cm of new tunnel in one minute.

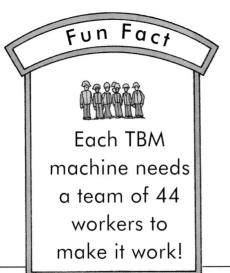

Fun Fact

Each TBM machine needs a team of 44 workers to make it work!

Tower cranes

Cranes lift heavy things. Tower cranes work on building sites. They can lift heavy loads up to the top of the tallest buildings.

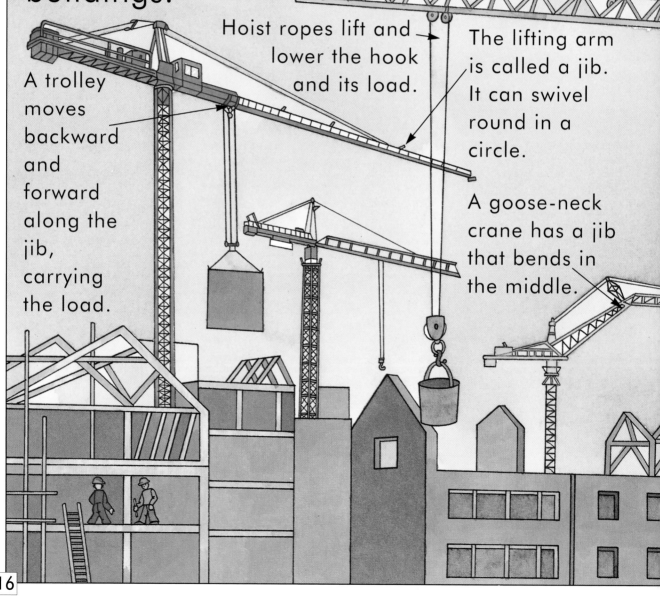

Hoist ropes lift and lower the hook and its load.

The lifting arm is called a jib. It can swivel round in a circle.

A trolley moves backward and forward along the jib, carrying the load.

A goose-neck crane has a jib that bends in the middle.

There is a big block of concrete at one end to stop the crane tipping over when it is picking up a heavy load.

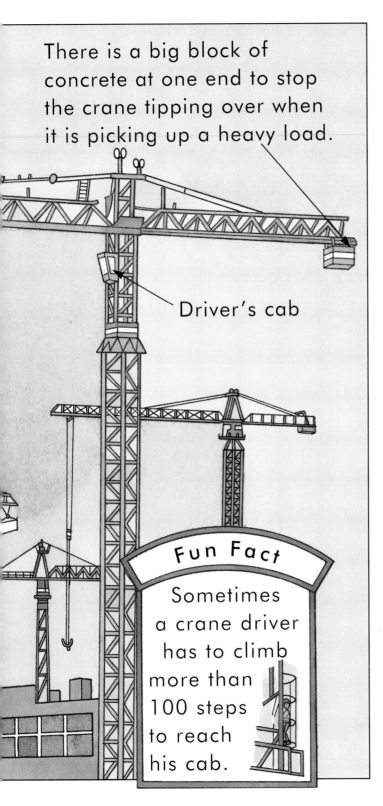

Driver's cab

Fun Fact

Sometimes a crane driver has to climb more than 100 steps to reach his cab.

Hoists

Hoists are used for lifting.

A **beam hoist** can lift a window frame into place.

This hoist carries people and materials in a cage to the top of a tall building.

Access platforms lift workers into the air in a safety cage.

Traveling cranes

Some cranes are mounted on trucks or crawler tracks. This means they can travel from one place to another.

Truck crane
Heavy truck cranes have several sets of big wheels to carry their weight.

The boom opens up like a telescope.

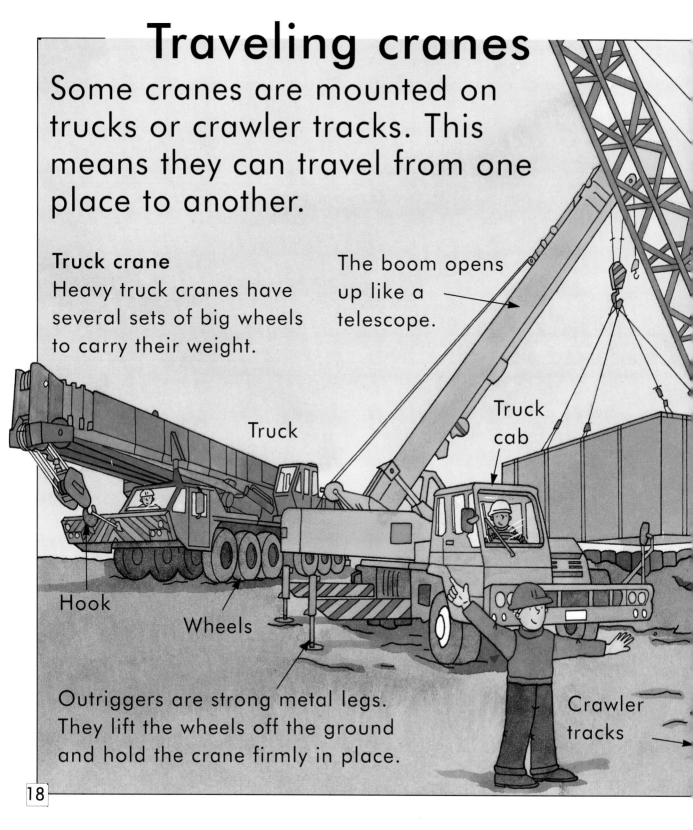

Truck

Truck cab

Hook

Wheels

Outriggers are strong metal legs. They lift the wheels off the ground and hold the crane firmly in place.

Crawler tracks

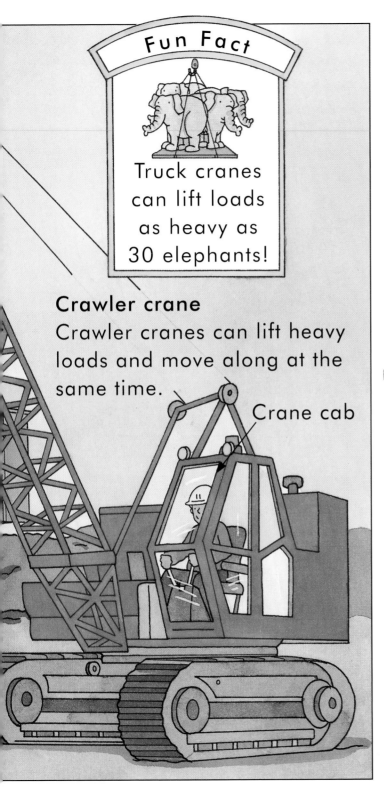
Crawler crane

Crawler cranes can lift heavy loads and move along at the same time.

Crane cab

Crane controls

Hand levers and foot pedals are used to do these things:

Lift and lower the boom and the hook.

Swing the crane round.

The crane operator can see all round through the windows.

Cranes in factories

Traveling cranes are used in some factories. They are fixed above the factory floor and move backward, forward, and sideway along rails.

This crane can lift a whole railroad car.

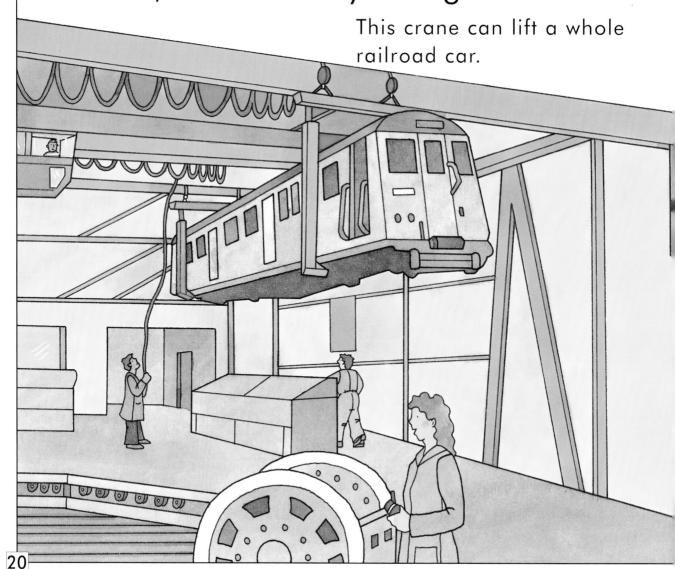

The manipulator on the end of this crane lifts machinery off a conveyor onto a trolley.

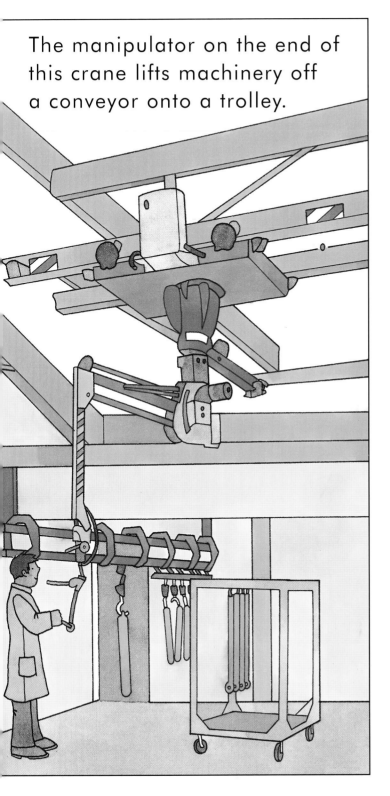

Special lifting jobs

This crane has been specially made to lift and carry a bucket of hot molten metal.

This crane lifts and carries metal by picking it up with a very strong magnet.

A frame with special lifting pads can pick up and carry a huge sheet of heavy glass.

Floating cranes

Floating crane vessels work at sea. This one is building an offshore oil rig. It has two booms that lift parts into place.

Crane

Oil rig

Hooks

Fun Fact

Floating cranes can even lift a ship out of the water!

About 350 people live and work on a floating crane vessel.

Boom

Helicopter

Helipad

Deck

There is a restaurant, movie theater and hospital on board.

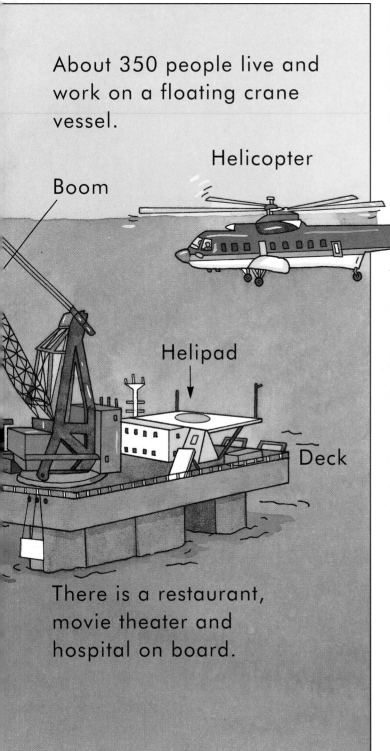

Huge **propellers** power the floating crane. It sails from one job to the next.

Helicopters carry workers and supplies to the oil rig and crane.

Smaller **floating cranes** are used to load and unload cargo ships when they are in harbor.

Index

Edited by Nicola Wright and Dee Turner
Consultant; Andrew Woodward
Design Manager; Kate Buxton
Printed in China

ISBN 1 84138 657 X

10 9 8 7 6 5 4 3 2 1

This edition first published in 2003 by
Chrysalis Children's Books
The Chrysalis Building, Bramley Rd, London W10 6SP

Copyright © Chrysalis Books PLC

24